Pesky Houseflies

Mary Elizabeth Salzmann

Consulting Editor, Diane Craig, M.A./Reading Specialist

A Division of ABDO

ABDO
Publishing Company

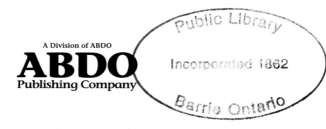

visit us at www.abdopublishing.com

Published by ABDO Publishing Company, a division of ABDO, P.O. Box 398166, Minneapolis, Minnesota 55439.
Copyright © 2012 by Abdo Consulting Group, Inc. International copyrights reserved in all countries. No part
of this book may be reproduced in any form without written permission from the publisher. SandCastle™ is a
trademark and logo of ABDO Publishing Company.

Printed in the United States of America, North Mankato, Minnesota
102011
012012

 PRINTED ON RECYCLED PAPER

Editor: Katherine Hengel
Content Developer: Nancy Tuminelly
Cover and Interior Design and Production: Kelly Doudna, Mighty Media, Inc.
Photo Credit: Shutterstock

Library of Congress Cataloging-in-Publication Data

Salzmann, Mary Elizabeth, 1968-
 Pesky houseflies / Mary Elizabeth Salzmann.
   p. cm. -- (Bug books)
 ISBN 978-1-61783-194-2
 1. Housefly--Juvenile literature. I. Title.
 QL537.M8S25 2012
 595.77'4--dc23
                    2011023418

SandCastle™ Level: Transitional

SandCastle™ books are created by a team of professional educators, reading specialists, and content
developers around five essential components—phonemic awareness, phonics, vocabulary, text
comprehension, and fluency—to assist young readers as they develop reading skills and strategies and
increase their general knowledge. All books are written, reviewed, and leveled for guided reading, early reading
intervention, and Accelerated Reader® programs for use in shared, guided, and independent reading and
writing activities to support a balanced approach to literacy instruction. The SandCastle™ series has four levels
that correspond to early literacy development. The levels are provided to help teachers and parents select
appropriate books for young readers.

Emerging Readers
(no flags)

Beginning Readers
(1 flag)

Transitional Readers
(2 flags)

Fluent Readers
(3 flags)

Contents

Pesky Houseflies

Houseflies are gray and black. They have dark stripes.

Houseflies have red eyes.
Their eyes are very big.

The **female's** eyes are far apart. The **male's** eyes are close together.

Flies have two short, thick **antennae**.

Houseflies have two wings. They fly about 5 miles per hour (8 kph).

A housefly's feet have tiny claws and hairs on them. That's how they walk on **ceilings!**

Houseflies have six legs. They can taste with the hairs on their legs.

Houseflies eat anything that rots. They also eat animal and **human** waste.

Houseflies live near people. Sometimes one will come inside to look for food!

Find the Housefly

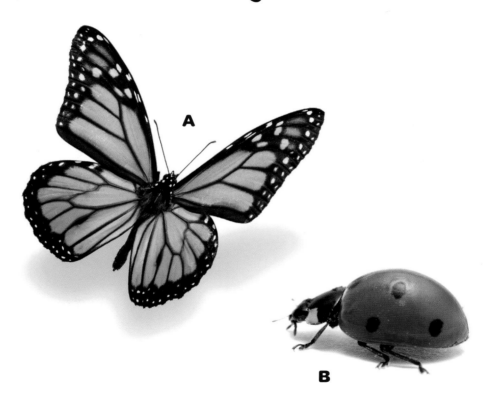

A

B

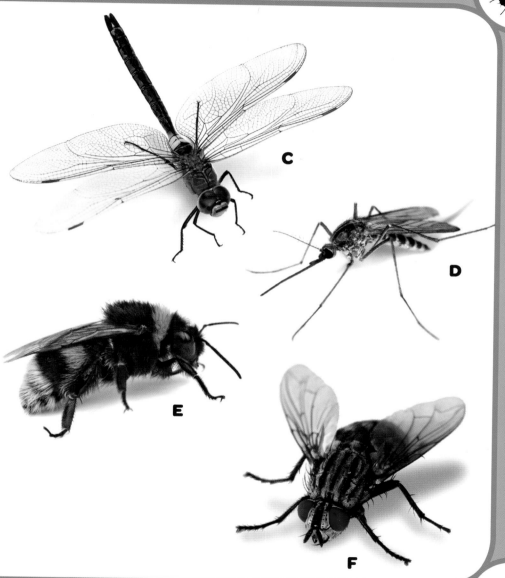

C

D

E

F

Glossary

antenna – a feeler on an insect's head.

ceiling – the upper surface or lining of a room.

female – being of the sex that can produce eggs or give birth. Mothers are female.

human – like or from a person.

male – being of the sex that can father offspring. Fathers are male.